Still I Bloom

Poems of Healing, Becoming, and Quiet Strength

Deborah Jefferson

DEDICATION

To every woman who has ever been broken and thought the pieces were all that remained
This is for you.
May you see that even in the shattering, beauty is being formed.
May you find the courage to become again,
the strength to break free,
and the grace to bloom in places you never imagined possible.

With love and purpose,
Deborah Jefferson

CONTENTS

Becoming Exploring growth, faith, and inner strength

The Sore is No More

Waterfall

The Flow

Power of Prayer

Superpower

Unshakeable Journey

The King's Ransom

Breaking Navigating heartbreak, choices, and transformation

Romantic Advances

If I Ever Get Married Again

Decisions You Made

Over Exposure

Peace

Chosen

Live Out Loud

Too Much Stuff

Blooming Embracing self-worth, purpose, and celebration

Be True

Get to Know Me

The Mission

I Am Enough

Becoming Her / She is the Embodiment of Her

Contemplating Thoughts

The Glow

Celebrate Yourself

ACKNOWLEDGMENTS

A heartfelt thank you to my family, friends, and mentors for your unwavering support and belief in me.

To every woman on her journey of discovery—this book is for you.

With love and gratitude,

Deborah Jefferson

Becoming

Before the bloom, there is the breaking of the ground. "Becoming" is the quiet work, the stretching, the rooting, the unseen growth that happens beneath the surface. It's where faith is tested, where identity is shaped, and where strength begins to whisper its presence.

In this section, the poems carry you through prayer, resilience, and the steady reminder that even when life feels hidden in the dark soil, something powerful is taking root. Becoming is not the end—it is the beginning of everything.

The Sore is No More

While on this healing journey, I got a new sore. It hurts so good I kept scratching for more
When you get that scab, it starts itching real good
You start scratching even though you know you shouldn't
Resist the itch
You're stronger than this
Leave it alone and let it be
You see
Some take longer than others to heal
Especially if we don't deal
with it
The hurt the shame the guilt
It's part of the healing process
The joy the peace the progress
It takes time to fully recover
But one day you'll soon discover
That the sore
Is no more.

Waterfall

Yeah, I remember when TLC said don't go chasing waterfalls.
Please stick to the rivers and the lakes that you're used to. I know
that you're gonna have it your way or nothing at all don't you
think you're moving too fast
We're not all running the same race
Not everyone's even going to the same place
You're trying to reach your peak while she's trying to go back to
her childhood to figure out why she only likes hood ninjas, and
he's trying to figure out what went wrong with him and his
momma
So, he can stop treating women like trash and treat us like the
queens that we are
We are goddesses and should be treated as such, don't we deserve
that much
But are we demanding the respect and the love that we so desire or
are we just settling for mediocre
And men, don't you want to be loved and honored as you flow
through the lakes and the rivers of life
Take your time and ride the tides, but hold on tight because the
direction of the current can change
And like the waterfalls
Life never stops flowing

The Flow

Unorganized
Striving to get some consistency in life
Things are in disarray
But it won't always be this way

I ask myself, "has it been like this before
And I am reminded of a time or two
Constantly looking for more
Enticed by the new

But keeping the old
I'm nostalgic like that
I never want to fold
Sometimes I wear too many hats

It's not about filling your cup to the rim
There should be a constant flow
When new things come in
Some things should go

Everything has its time in place
For the reason or the season
Flow at a steady pace
With a heavy progression

Contemplating Thoughts

As I sit here contemplating
on the thoughts going through my head
I took the wrong directions
To reach my destination
So many wrong turns
I didn't know which way to go
The only thing left to do was run
Only this time I was running alone
For the first time in my life in the wilderness
All on my own

As I sit here contemplating
On the thoughts going through my head
When I think of my thought process
I should've taken a recess
But nevertheless
I thought that freedom was my rest
Although there were many sleepless nights
With time I progressed
Even when pain reignites
I am no longer oppressed

Power of Prayer

Devil you're not gonna stop me
I got to get this book up out of me
Regurgitate what was taken from me
You stole what was rightfully mine
With thorns intertwined
Peeking through the vines
Covered so beautifully
Designed specifically
Undoubtedly, a conspiracy
To take me out
I have no doubt
What it was all about
But there was a lamb
Reminding me of who's I am
Telling me about the plan
Giving me strength to endure
Keeping my heart pure
My spirit you tried to lure
But you see I'm an heir
You can put me anywhere
I'll always make it with the power of prayer

Superpower

Silence is her superpower
Being strong enough to devour
Everything that surrounds her

A force so powerful
It becomes influential
Better yet consequential

It overpowers her
Like a strong tower
Getting stronger by the hour

Silence is her superpower
A beacon of light from the watch tower
Shining in the dark hour

In the quiet of the night
She decides to invite
Her friend contrite

She is consumed
With having to exclude
Herself from doom

Silence is her superpower
It can be a peculiar power
Even undisputed power

She has been through the fire
While it doesn't define her
In some ways it guides her

Down different pathways
We were taught to look both ways
In the silence look towards the flames

Silence is her superpower
Being strong enough to devour
Everything that surrounds her

Unshakable Journey

Sometimes I need time to recharge
a lot of times I'm putting on a façade
We're all taught to put our best foot forward
Never moving backwards
I stay focused on the future
Building my tomorrow
Like a suture
I'm immovable, unstoppable
Climbing over every obstacle
Unshakable, unbreakable
Refusing to fall
With every waking moment
My feet are on the ground
Claiming my dream
I don't have to chase
Just keeping a steady pace
Because it's a journey
Not a race

The Kings Ransom

If this is something real, then it won't go away, nor will it happen in a defiled way
I know where my blessings come from, and they come in the purest form
This can be a test or a glimpse into the future
A life worth having is worth waiting for
The woman I am now is worth fighting for,
And who I can become is so much more there's a purpose for my life
My father ordered my steps and prepared a pathway to the life, he desires for me
A life that will bring him glory
This life is not to be played with
And in his timing, he will bring my king to walk alongside me
To carry me when needed
Until then I will wait patiently until he has been ransomed

Breaking

To break is human. "Breaking" is the part of the journey where love, loss, and life collide. It's the place where choices cut deep, where hearts feel exposed, and where the weight of letting go feels heavier than holding on.

But breaking is not destruction, it is transformation. In these poems, you'll feel the ache of endings, the rawness of vulnerability, and the cracks where the light begins to seep in. Breaking prepares the soul for its greatest bloom.

Romantic Advances

Thrill seeker, dreamer
On this pathway to nowhere
Who is leading her
She must be going somewhere

Will she allow someone to come with
Go along for the ride
They may need a locksmith
To get inside

Her heart no one will ever reach
It's been frozen into a block of ice
In the system theirs been a breach
Of trust that was compromised

So, she's still a bit cautious
But she likes to take chances
Sometimes feeling nauseous
When someone makes romantic advances

If I Ever Get Married Again

If I ever get married again
We're dating the whole way through
Every encounter is going to be like someone new
We don't even have to live together seven days a week
We can text all night and make plans to see each other once
or twice a week
I want to miss you so bad but have butterflies when I know
we're getting together
Testing the waters with you liquidizes
But never drowns in a sea of displeasure
I am mesmerized by the temptation
Oftentimes just thinking, contemplating
On the what ifs, when wills
Then I'm reminded of the right now
And I ask myself how
Can I let my guard down
Will it shatter like breaking glass
Or will it rise and surpass
Every obstacle known to man
If ever get married again

Decisions You Made

Sometimes you just want a quiet moment
just time to yourself
even if it's just sitting outside in the car that you can't even drive
anymore
but still yours
or just going to the store,
not really shopping just being around people kind of sort of
Getting out of the house
looking at something else other than the same walls, the same
carpet, the same everything every day
Making time to play in the rain
It's okay to create a storm or two
So, life doesn't become mundane
And you wake up one day
wondering why you are where you are
and why you chose the decisions that you made.

Overexposure

What do you want from me
What is it that you seek
What are you pleading for
Is it my allure
Clearly, there's a disconnect
I can't seem to dissect
The real desire
Figure out what's fueling the fire
Fanning the flames
Of this volcanic explosion
As the eruption transpires
Spilling over
Spreading out onto the surface
Overexposure

Peace

All I want is peace
But do I have to go on island alone
they say no man is an island,
but when I share my world
Those true colors are shown
They remain hidden for a while
Then the rainbow explodes
But there is no pot of gold

All I want is peace
Is that too much to ask

Isolation can't be the key
I refuse to live in complete solitude
Although at times it is needed
We all need time for ourselves
To reflect on the past
and figure out the next

All I want is peace
Isn't that the goal
Money can't buy it
Man or woman can't give it or take it away
We serve the Prince of Peace
Keep your mind focused on him
He will wash away all your cares
And give you a peace like no one else can

Chosen

I am chosen by the one who saves
He created me in his image
In his hands he molded a ball of clay
And turned it into a masterpiece

I am chosen for a divine purpose
He already knew my name
before my mother
knew I was in her womb

I am chosen for greatness
I am a king's daughter
I have royalty flowing through my blood
The ultimate sacrifice was made

I am chosen to walk in purpose
I am chosen to shine a light
I am chosen to be a vessel
I am chosen to walk upright

With my head held high
And to boldly speak before you
Sharing the thoughts that I
Have been sent to share with you

Live Out Loud

It's time to come outside
But you gotta take off all the layers
You've been carrying all this weight,
hiding it from the naysayers
The guilt, the shame, the heartache and pain
Stand outside and let it wash away in the rain
It's time to come outside
And let your face rise to the sun
Stand tall and walk boldly
You no longer have to run
It's time to live out loud

Too Much Stuff

You got too much stuff
it's time to unpack
Go through some things
and figure out what's what
You kept them hidden for so long
You walk around with your mask on
Like you don't have all this stuff
Buried deep inside
Piles and piles
Can you even, see?
Do you know the way out?
You got too much stuff
Why are you holding onto it?
Ashes, to ashes and dust to dust
Load it up and put it on a truck
And send it away
To never-never land
That's where things go
Even if you don't understand
You can no longer keep them inside
Although that might have been your plan
You can't erase the past
Everything you've been carrying
Has gotten way too heavy
You weren't built for that
He said your burden will be light
and your yoke will be easy
Cast your cares upon him
He can carry the load
Just start unpacking
Even though it may be rough
You must realize
you got too much stuff

Blooming

After the soil and the storm comes the rising.
"Blooming" is the moment you remember who you are—rooted, radiant, and resilient. It's where self-worth takes shape, where joy returns, and where the glow of healing cannot be hidden.

These poems celebrate the journey of becoming her—the woman who knows her value, honors her story, and dares to live out loud. Blooming is not perfection—it is proof that no matter what tried to bury you, you were always meant to rise.

Be True

When I'm done, I'm done, no need to drag it on
the best thing for me to do is to move on
It took a while for me to get this point, but I know this decision is
on point
You tried to break me
As if you had made me
But I was created in his image,
I was created for greatness
You can't destroy a masterpiece
you can't take my peace
I'm on a journey
I have a yearning
To be whole
To be free of all the debris
that I picked up along the way
This time I can't stray away
from all the goodness that's coming my way
I can't afford to play
childish games
Because the result will always be the same
It's time to change the narrative
It is imperative
In order to do the good that you were created to do
You have to be true to you

Get To Know Me

I knew that it was no longer beneficial to me
In such a way that it was detrimental to me
I could feel it through every fiber of me
But I kept striving to be
This whole version of me
That I was never meant to be
You see
You had your own image of me
Of what you wanted me to be
I knew I had to be set free
Free to see what I could be
Free to be who I'm supposed to be
I'm learning there's so much more to me
If I just take the time and get to know me

The Mission

They say an idle mind is the devil's playground
Keep looking and God only knows what you'll find
But were you even searching for anything or just keeping busy
Focusing on your goals trying to reach your destiny
But in the meantime, in between time, you were still longing for some me-time
To get you through the hard times, the dark times, the low times, even the high times
That little piece of Heaven that was so sinful
It spoke to the selfish nature that was hidden within you
Lying dormant within your subconscious
Ready to break free from bondage
Sneak out from behind the shadows
And come to fruition
Was this really the mission

I Am Enough

I am enough
Enough to fill your cup with joy
I am enough
Enough to build not destroy
I am enough
Enough to know when to deploy
I am enough
Enough to know I didn't need old boy
I am enough
Enough to know not to self-destroy
I am enough
Enough to know that I am not a toy
I am enough
Enough to fill my own cup with joy

Living in Your Truth

Thoughts of me
Thoughts of she
Thoughts of who I'm supposed to be

Thoughts of what
Thoughts of when
Thoughts of where my life begins

Thoughts of how
Thoughts of now
Thoughts of oh wow

Thoughts of you
Thoughts of ooh
Thoughts of living in your truth

She Is the Embodiment of Her

She is the embodiment of her
Clothed in a strength that can't be seen with the human eye
Brimming with a light that illuminates so bright

She is the embodiment of her
A quiet place during a storm
That is stirring up something so brilliant
It transforms

She is the embodiment of her
Drawn up out of the miry clay
With a song of hallelujah and praise

She is the embodiment of her
Walking boldly in her essence
Without fear or hesitation

She is the embodiment of her
Not trying to be outspoken
Yet she has the loudest whisper

Concealing Scars

Trust in the lord, with all your heart
Keep his words close
So that you will never depart
In times of trouble
The Lord your God
Is amazingly dependable
Do not be deceived
By the words of a foe
Or what appears to be a sheep
Clothed in a fabric so light
With the slightest touch
Piercing like a knife
Go to your father for healing
He will take care of your wounds
While shielding
Your scars he's concealing

The Glow

Shine bright
Own your light
You have every right

Stand Tall
Embrace it all
You don't have to play it small

Rise above
All you've ever thought of
Never fall short of

The gift and glow
For you to sow
A seed to grow

Celebrate Yourself

Celebrate yourself
for all that you've done
All that you are
All that you've won

Celebrate yourself
For getting' back up
when you've been knocked down
And remembering to wear your crown

Celebrate yourself
For dropping that cape
and losing weight
It's never too late

Celebrate yourself
For no reason at all,
or the simple fact
that you stood tall

Celebrate yourself
through the highs and lows
And all the bumpy roads
With the heavier loads

Celebrate yourself
For committing to you
And not wondering who
will be there for you

Celebrate yourself
For passing the test
And recognizing

that you are the best

About the Author: Deborah Jefferson

Deborah Jefferson is a multifaceted author, life coach, and CEO of Harobeds Thoughts, an organization dedicated to personal growth, healing, and self-improvement. She weaves her faith, resilience, and passion for storytelling into every project, creating works that inspire and empower.

With a strong focus on helping others through their healing journeys, Deborah shares her story with authenticity and vulnerability, guiding readers toward self-discovery and transformation. Her writing spans multiple genres, including poetry, self-help, and memoir.

Deborah is the visionary behind the Our Words Matter Black Author's Expo, a platform celebrating diverse voices and stories. She also hosts the podcast *Sharing Your Story and Conversations That Heal*, amplifying narratives of strength and hope.

When she's not writing or mentoring, Deborah is crafting meaningful projects like her journal, Believe in Yourself Sis. Through her poetry collection Still I Bloom Poems of Blooming, Healing, and Quiet Strength, Deborah captures the essence of womanhood, resilience, and the journey to self-love.

Deborah resides in South Carolina and continues to inspire others through her words and her unwavering belief that healing and growth are within everyone's reach.

Connect with me on social media

YouTube Harobeds Thoughts

Facebook Harobeds Thoughts

TikTok Harobeds Thoughts

www.harobedsthoughts.com

www.ingramcontent.com/pod-product-compliance
Lightning Source LLC
Chambersburg PA
CBHW071803040426
42446CB00012B/2696